AMAZING ANIMALS OF THE WORLD ③

Volume 1

Abalone, Black — Butterfly, Giant Swallowtail

GROLIER

an imprint of

Scholastic Library Publishing

www.scholastic.com/librarypublishing

WITHDRAWN

First published 2006 by Grolier, an imprint of Scholastic Library Publishing

For information address the publisher: Grolier, Scholastic Library Publishing
90 Old Sherman Turnpike
Danbury, CT 06816

10 digit: Set ISBN: 0-7172-6179-4; Volume ISBN: 0-7172-6180-8
13 digit: Set ISBN: 978-0-7172-6179-6; Volume ISBN: 978-0-7172-6180-2

Printed and bound in the U.S.A.

Library of Congress Cataloging-in-Publications Data:
Amazing animals of the world 3.
p.cm.
Includes indexes.
Contents: v. 1. Abalone, Black–Butterfly, Giant Swallowtail -- v. 2. Butterfly, Indian Leaf–Dormouse, Garden -- v. 3. Duck, Ferruginous–Glassfish, Indian -- v. 4. Glider, Sugar–Isopod, Freshwater -- v. 5. Jackal, Side-Striped–Margay -- v. 6. Markhor–Peccary, Collared -- v. 7. Pelican, Brown–Salamander, Spotted -- v. 8. Salamander, Two Lined–Spider, Barrel -- v. 9. Spider, Common House–Tuna, Albacore -- v. 10. Tunicate, Light-Bulb–Zebra, Grevy's.
ISBN 0–7172–6179–4 (set : alk. paper) -- ISBN 0–7172–6180–8 (v. 1 : alk. paper) -- ISBN 0-7172-6181–6 (v. 2 : alk. paper) -- ISBN 0-7172-6182–4 (v. 3 : alk. paper) -- ISBN 0-7172-6183–2 (v. 4 : alk. paper) -- ISBN 0-7172-6184–0 (v. 5 : alk. paper) -- ISBN 0-7172-6185–9 (v. 6 : alk. paper) -- ISBN 0-7172-6186–7 (v. 7 : alk. paper) -- ISBN 0-7172-6187–5 (v. 8 : alk. paper) -- ISBN 0-7172-6188–3 (v. 9 : alk. paper) -- ISBN 0-7172-6189–1 (v. 10 : alk.paper)
1. Animals--Juvenile literature. I. Grolier (Firm) II. Title: Amazing animals of the world three.
QL49.A455 2006
590—dc22
2006010870

About This Set

Amazing Animals of the World 3 brings you pictures of 400 exciting creatures, and important information about how and where they live.

Each page shows just one species, or individual type, of animal. They all fall into seven main categories, or groups, of animals (classes and phylums scientifically) identified on each page with an icon (picture)—amphibians, arthropods, birds, fish, mammals, other invertebrates, and reptiles. Short explanations of what these group names mean, and other terms used commonly in the set, appear on page 4 in the Glossary.

Scientists use all kinds of groupings to help them sort out the types of animals that exist today and once wandered the earth (extinct species). *Kingdoms*, *classes*, *phylums*, *genus*, and *species* are among the key words here that are also explained in the Glossary.

Where animals live is important to know as well. Each of the species in this set lives in a particular place in the world, which you can see outlined on the map on each page. And in those places, the animals tend to favor a particular habitat—an environment the animal finds suitable for life—with food, shelter, and safety from predators that might eat it. There they also find ways to coexist with other animals in the area that might eat somewhat different food, use different homes, and so on.

Each of the main habitats is named on the page and given an icon, or picture, to help you envision it. The habitat names are further defined in the Glossary on page 4.

As well as being part of groups like species, animals fall into other categories that help us understand their lives or behavior. You will find these categories in the Glossary on page 4, where you will learn about carnivores, herbivores, and other types of animals.

And there is more information you might want about an animal—its size, diet, where it lives, and how it carries on its species—the way it creates its young. All these facts and more appear in the data boxes at the top of each page.

Finally, the set is arranged alphabetically by the most common name of the species. That puts most beetles, for example, together in a group so you can compare them easily.

But some animals' names are not so common, and they don't appear near others like them. For instance, the chamois is a kind of goat or antelope. To find animals that are similar—or to locate any species—look in the Index at the end of each book in the set (pages 45–48). It lists all animals by their various names (you will find the Giant South American River Turtle under Turtle, Giant South American River, and also under its other name—Arrau). And you will find all birds, fish, and so on gathered under their broader groupings.

Similarly, smaller like groups appear in the Set Index as well—butterflies include swallowtails and blues, for example.

Table of Contents
Volume 1

Glossary

Amphibians—species usually born from eggs in water or wet places, which change (metamorphose) into land animals. Frogs and salamanders are typical. They breathe through their skin mainly and have no scales.

Arctic and Antarctic—icy, cold, dry areas at the ends of the globe that lack trees but see small plants grown in thawed areas (tundra). Penguins and seals are common inhabitants.

Arthropods—animals with segmented bodies, hard outer skin, and jointed legs, such as spiders and crabs.

Birds—born from eggs, these creatures have wings and often can fly. Eagles, pigeons, and penguins are all birds, though penguins cannot fly through the air.

Carnivores—they are animals that eat other animals. Many species do eat each other sometimes, and a few eat dead animals. Lions kill their prey and eat it, while vultures clean up dead bodies of animals.

Cities, Towns, and Farms—places where people live and have built or used the land and share it with many species. Sometimes these animals live in human homes or just nearby.

Class—part or division of a phylum.

Deserts—dry, often warm areas where animals often are more active on cooler nights or near water sources. Owls, scorpions, and jack rabbits are common in American deserts.

Endangered—some animals in this set are marked as endangered because it is possible they will become extinct soon.

Extinct—these species have died out altogether for whatever reason.

Family—part of an order.

Fish—water animals (aquatic) that typically are born from eggs and breathe through gills. Trout and eels are fish, though whales and dolphins are not (they are mammals).

Forests and Mountains—places where evergreen (coniferous) and leaf-shedding (deciduous) trees are common, or that rise in elevation to make cool, separate habitats. Rain forests are different. (see Rain forests)

Fresh Water—lakes, rivers, and the like carry fresh water (unlike Oceans and Shores, where the water is salty). Fish and birds abound, as do insects, frogs, and mammals.

Genus—part of a family.

Grasslands—habitats with few trees and light rainfall. Grasslands often lie between forests and deserts, and they are home to birds, coyotes, antelope, and snakes, as well as many other kinds of animals.

Herbivores—these animals eat mainly plants. Typically they are hoofed animals (ungulates) that are common on grasslands, such as antelope or deer. Domestic (nonwild) ones are cows and horses.

Hibernators—species that live in harsh areas with very cold winters slow down their functions then and sort of sleep through the hard times.

Invertebrates—animals that lack backbones or internal skeletons. Many, such as insects and shrimp, have hard outer coverings. Clams and worms are also invertebrates.

Kingdom—the largest division of species. Commonly there are understood to be five kingdoms: animals, plants, fungi, protists, and monerans.

Mammals—these creatures usually bear live young and feed them on milk from the mother. A few lay eggs (monotremes like the platypus) or nurse young in a pouch (marsupials like opossums and kangaroos).

Migrators—some species spend different seasons in different places, moving to where more food, warmth, or safety can be found. Birds often do this, sometimes over long distances, but other types of animals also move seasonally, including fish and mammals.

Oceans and Shores—seawater is salty, often deep, and huge. In it live many fish, invertebrates, and even some mammals, such as whales. On the shore, birds and other creatures often gather.

Order—part of a class.

Phylum—part of a kingdom.

Rain forests—here huge trees grow among many other plants helped by the warm, wet environment. Thousands of species of animals also live in these rich habitats.

Reptiles—these species have scales, lungs to breathe, and lay eggs or give birth to live young. Dinosaurs are thought to have been reptiles, while today the class includes turtles, snakes, lizards, and crocodiles.

Scientific name—the genus and species name of a creature in Latin. For instance, Canis lupus is the wolf. Scientific names avoid the confusion possible with common names in any one language or across languages.

Species—a group of the same type of living thing. Part of an order.

Subspecies—a variant but quite similar part of a species.

Territorial—many animals mark out and defend a patch of ground as their home area. Birds and mammals may call quite small or quite large spots their territories.

Vertebrates—animals with backbones and skeletons under their skins

Black Abalone
Haliotis cracherodii

Length: 5 to 6 inches
Diet: seaweed
Home: Pacific Coast of North America from Monterey to Baja California

Method of Reproduction: egg layer
Order: Primitive snail-like mollusks
Family: Abalones

 Oceans and Shores

 Other Invertebrates

© WILLIAM E. TOWNSEND, JR. / PHOTO RESEARCHERS

The black abalone makes its home along the rugged Pacific seashore. It lives on rocks and in crevices in between the high-tide and the low-tide lines. This is a perfect home for the black abalone, because it feasts on the seaweed that gets washed up by the waves. Of all the abalones in California, the black abalone strays farthest from the low-tide line. By keeping to the high rocks, it avoids being eaten by octopuses and fish. But its open perch also leaves it vulnerable to sea gulls and other land predators—including human beachcombers.

The abalone differs from most other snail-like mollusks in that it has a row of holes in its shell. It uses these holes to pass a steady stream of water over its gills. As abalones grow, their shells form new holes, and the older holes gradually close up. The hole closest to the edge of an abalone shell is always the newest. The one farthest from the edge is the next one to close up.

Black abalones lay their eggs in August and September. They release the eggs directly into the water at high tide. The eggs then drift freely until they hatch. The young abalones also drift. About a month after they are born, the tiny abalones—only about $\frac{1}{25}$th of an inch long—settle onto the sea bottom. They grow to about an inch the first year. Eventually the waves wash a growing abalone onto a rocky shore. There it will attach itself with its single, muscular foot.

5

Death Adder
Acanthophis antarcticus

Length: up to 2½ feet
Diet: small mammals, birds, and lizards
Home: Australia, New Guinea, and nearby Pacific islands

Number of Young: up to 20
Order: Snakes and lizards
Family: Cobras, kraits, and coral snakes

Forests and Mountains

Reptiles

© MICHAEL & PATRICIA FOGDEN / CORBIS

As its name suggests, the death adder is one of the world's deadliest snakes. But it is not a true adder or even closely related to one. The two kinds of snakes look very much alike and live in similar woodland homes. However, you could see the difference between true adders and the death adder by inspecting their fangs. Adders and other vipers have movable fangs. But the fangs of the death adder are fixed in one position.

Death adders sleep during the day and hunt at night. These snakes do not chase their prey. Instead, they wait in ambush. The death adder's color and markings make it difficult to see in the sand. The snake further disguises itself by coiling up and partially burying itself. As it waits for its prey, the death adder may stick its tail out of the sand and wiggle it. When a curious mouse or lizard scurries up to inspect this wiggling lure, the death adder strikes. The snake bites fiercely and then swallows its prey whole. In a single bite, a death adder can inject enough venom to kill three human beings.

Death adders do not need to eat very often. They do not burn a lot of calories because they are not very active. They save even more energy because they are cold-blooded. Cold-blooded animals, such as snakes and other reptiles, do not burn energy to keep their bodies warm. Instead, they absorb the warmth they need by basking in the sun.

Puff Adder
Bitis arietans

Length: 3 to 5 feet
Diet: rodents and amphibians
Home: Africa south of the Sahara and around the Red Sea

Number of Young: up to 40
Order: Lizards and snakes
Family: Vipers
Suborder: Snakes

 Grasslands

 Reptiles

© MICHAEL FOGDEN / BRUCE COLEMAN INC.

Puff adders are feared everywhere in the African savanna, from south of the Sahara Desert to the Cape of Good Hope. They are found in mountains at altitudes of up to 6,500 feet. The only place they do not live is in tropical rain forests. Because they are so common and have such a deadly poison, they are the most feared snakes in Africa. Humans can die within 24 hours of being bitten. But the adder does not attack humans if it is not in direct danger.

The effect of the poison works very quickly on the adder's prey, mostly amphibians and rodents. If bitten by the adder's long fangs, a rat is seriously injured and quickly dies while trying to escape. Even if its prey escapes, the snake will follow it, sometimes in the darkest night. The snake can smell its prey's trail with a sense organ located on its tongue. Hidden by its camouflage, the puff adder often surprises animals traveling through the savanna. It bites them on the nose when they are grazing, without giving them a chance to escape.

The puff adder has a large, triangular head. The poison glands are located there. Its fangs are among the longest of any snake's. Its heavy body is as thick as a man's arm. To make it look even scarier, when the adder is in danger, it whistles, raises its head, and breathes in air to puff its body up to twice its normal size. This is how it got its name.

Black-Browed Albatross
Diomedia melanophris

Length: 32 to 38 inches
Weight: about 7½ pounds
Diet: fish, squid, and other
  marine animals
Number of Eggs: 1

Home: oceans south of Tropic
  of Capricorn
Order: Tubenoses
Family: Albatrosses

  Oceans and Shores

Birds

© WOLFGANG KAEHLER / CORBIS

The long, dark stripe of feathers above the eyes of the black-browed albatross gives the bird a frowning, almost scowling, expression. Long ago, Dutch sailors nicknamed this medium-size albatross the *mollymawk,* meaning "silly gull." It was so named for its awkward way of walking. When chased, this albatross tries to run, but usually ends up tripping and falling over its enormous wings. The bird's wingspan is over seven feet.

Like other albatrosses, this species is an excellent flier. Its long, strong wings enable it to glide effortlessly over the ocean waves for hours, even days, at a time. The albatross is also a good swimmer. When the winds are still, it settles on the water and rides the slowly rolling waves. It catches fish and squid with its long, heavy bill, which has a sharp hook at the tip.

Like other albatrosses the blackbrow follows ships, looking for scraps and eating garbage that has been thrown overboard. This species is also active at night and often silently follows a ship in the moonlight. The black-browed albatross is said to be the boldest and friendliest member of its family. This seabird is almost fearless of people.

The albatrosses breed on deserted ocean islands and on barren sea cliffs in the southern oceans of the world. The mated pair tend their single egg and care for the hatchling. The threesome stay together for several months.

Waved Albatross
Diomedea irrorata

Length: 33 to 37 inches
Weight: about 8 pounds (male); about 6 pounds (female)
Diet: fish and squid

Number of Eggs: 1
Home: southeastern Pacific Ocean
Order: Tubenoses
Family: Albatrosses

 Oceans and Shores

 Birds

© WOLFGANG KAEHLER / CORBIS

Albatross are large ocean birds known for their spectacular gliding flights. From a distance, they are easily recognized by their long, narrow wings. Up close, one can see that they all have long, hooked bills with large, tubelike nostrils. Albatross, like other "tubenoses," have an excellent sense of smell, which they use to locate food floating near the surface of the ocean.

The waved albatross lives on the cold waters of the Peru Current in the southeastern Pacific Ocean. Except when nesting, it spends its entire life at sea, bobbing on the waves and scooping up fish and squid near the surface.

Waved albatross nest on two desert islands in the southeastern Pacific: the Isla de la Plata, off the coast of Ecuador, and Hood Island in the Galápagos. Before mating, the birds gather in groups to perform wild courtship dances. As they jump and flap their wings, they seem to laugh hysterically: "ha-ha-ha" and "whooo-ooo." After mating, waved albatross build no nests. The female simply lays her single egg on the bare ground among boulders and cacti.

Experts estimate that there are only 6,000 to 12,000 waved albatross today. The birds may be the last of a primitive form of ancient albatross known from fossils. At present, this small population is in no danger of extinction.

Two-Toed Amphiuma
Amphiuma means

Length: 14½ to 30 inches
Diet: worms, crustaceans, mollusks, insects, small fish, snakes, and frogs
Method of Reproduction: egg layer

Home: southeastern United States
Order: Salamanders and newts
Family: Amphiumas

Fresh Water

Amphibians

© FRED WHITEHEAD / ANIMALS ANIMALS / EARTH SCENES

With its long, skinny body, the two-toed amphiuma looks like an eel. Some people even call it the congo eel. But the amphiuma is really a salamander. It has tiny arms and legs. Each arm of the two-toed amphiuma has two fingers; each leg has two toes.

Another common name for the amphiuma is the ditch eel. It lives in ditches, ponds, swamps, small streams, and other aquatic habitats. It spends almost all of its life in the water. During the day the amphiuma usually hides among plants or debris at the bottom of the water. It is most active at night, when it crawls around looking for food. The slightest sign of danger will make the amphiuma rush back to its hiding place.

Its main weapon against enemies is its teeth. An amphiuma can inflict painful bites on a person who carelessly handles it.

Two-toed amphiuma mate in water, but the female lays her eggs in a moist spot on land. A large female may lay several hundred eggs. The eggs hatch into tiny larvae. Like other amphibians, amphiuma undergo metamorphosis, or change. But their metamorphosis is unusual because some body parts change and others do not. For example, the amphiuma's skin metamorphoses, but the creature never develops eyelids. Thus, an amphiuma keeps some of its larval characteristics while developing certain characteristics found only in adult amphibians.

Jewel Anemone
Corynactis sp.

Height: about 1¼ inches
Width: about 1 inch
Diet: plankton and other small marine animals
Methods of Reproduction: sexual and asexual

Home: coasts of Atlantic and Pacific oceans and Mediterranean Sea
Order: Corallimorpharia
Family: Corallimorphids

Oceans and Shores

Other Invertebrates

© JENNY & TONY ENDERBY / LONELY PLANET IMAGES

Despite their name, jewel anemones are not true sea anemones. They are more closely related to the stony corals. Their "jewels" are the gemlike knobs at the tips of their tentacles. These species are also commonly known as the club-tipped anemones.

Jewel anemones live close to shore along the coasts of Europe, North America, and eastern Asia. Along the coast of California, the anemones grow on rocks and pier pilings from the low-tide line to water depths of 95 feet. They occur in both quiet bays and wave-swept shores. The California club-tipped anemone, *C. californica*, is either red, pink, orange, purple, brown, or cream. Its tentacles are usually white. A very similar species, *C. viridis* (shown here), lives along European and Mediterranean shores.

Like true anemones, a jewel anemone attaches itself to a hard surface with the flat, sticky disk at the bottom of its stalklike body. But like corals, these creatures grow crowded together in colonies. The disk of one jewel anemone usually touches that of one or more neighbors.

The plump knob on the anemone's tentacles contain the largest stinging cells of any marine invertebrate. Despite their size, their sting does not pack much of a wallop to humans. The stingers are effective only against tiny creatures such as zooplankton.

Sable Antelope
Hippotragus niger

Length of the Body: 6½ to 8½ feet
Length of the Tail: 1½ to 2½ inches
Height at the Shoulder: 4 to 4¾ feet
Weight: 420 to 590 pounds
Diet: leaves and grasses

Number of Young: 1
Home: southeastern Africa
Order: Even-toed hoofed mammals
Family: Bovines
Subfamily: Roan and sable antelopes

 Grasslands

 Mammals

© WINIFRED WISNIEWSKI / FRANK LANE PICTURE AGENCY / CORBIS

? Endangered Animals

With its long, powerful horns, the sable antelope can defend itself from enemies—even lions! These bold antelope have been known to charge humans that dare come too close. Despite its bravery, the sable-antelope population is dwindling. The only large, healthy herds are found in national parks. Fortunately, the countries of Africa have several such parks, which draw many tourists each year.

Sadly, one type of sable antelope is endangered and may already be extinct. The giant sable antelope, *Hippotragus niger variani*, has been caught in the middle of a bloody civil war in the country of Angola. At last report, this magnificent animal survived in only two small areas. However, biologists have not been able to look for the large antelope because of the war.

Sable antelope live in herds led by a single male, or bull. The herds may also include 10 to 20 does and their young. Other males, the bachelors, form separate groups. The ruling bull in a mixed herd is kept busy chasing bachelor males away from his does.

When the does are ready to give birth, they leave the bull and gather with other pregnant females. The baby sable antelope are born between August and February, which is spring and summer in the Southern Hemisphere. The newborns weigh between 25 and 30 pounds, and nurse from their mothers for up to eight months.

Argiope
Argiope bruennichi

Length: ½ to ¾ inch (female);
⅛ to ¼ inch (male)
Method of Reproduction: egg
layer

Diet: insects
Home: southern Europe
Order: Spiders
Family: Orb-weavers

 Grasslands

 Arthropods

© J. C. CARTON / BRUCE COLEMAN INC.

The argiope, or orb-web spider, is common in southern Europe. Similar to America's common garden spider, the argiope rarely leaves the center of its web. It waits for its prey—insects of all kinds, and even large butterflies. Sometimes it hides near the web, waiting for an insect to be trapped in it.

The argiope has a golden-yellow belly with black horizontal stripes. Its web usually has a zigzag design that makes the web stronger and also warns birds and other animals of the fragile web's presence, so they can avoid it. The spider would have to rebuild the web if a bird flew though it.

The argiope needs a trap that will hold the weight of its prey as it struggles to free itself. The web must also stand up against bad weather. Periods of dryness and rain cause problems for the argiope's fragile home. You can often see spiders busily fixing their webs. If the argiope is disturbed during its work, it may drop to the ground on a dragline thread. It stays attached to the web by the thread and uses it to climb back up to the web.

You can watch the spider to predict weather. In nice and calm weather, it keeps working on the threads of its web or weaves another trap. If it stops working, it means that rain is not far off. As soon as the sun returns, the spider goes back to work.

Razorbilled Auk
Alca torda

Length: 16 to 18 inches
Weight: about 1½ pounds
Diet: fish, crustaceans, mollusks, and algae
Number of Eggs: usually 1

Home: northern Atlantic Ocean
Order: Water birds
Family: Auks

 Oceans and Shores

 Birds

© ROGER TIDMAN / CORBIS

It is no coincidence that the razorbilled auk resembles a penguin. Although the two types of birds are not closely related, they occupy very similar habitats. Penguins are the diving birds of the cold southern seas, while auks, such as the razorbill, fill this role in the far north. Penguins and razorbills are excellent swimmers and divers, using their wings like flippers under the water. They both walk upright. But unlike penguins, razorbills can fly. Rather than a flapping, up-and-down motion, these seabirds move their short wings as if swimming through the air.

The adult razorbilled auk is best recognized by the handsome white stripes on its large, flattened bill. In summer the bird has additional white lines running from its bill to each eye. Both sexes look similar. Chicks have a relatively smaller bill and lack their parents' white facial stripes.

Auks such as the razorbill spend most of the year at sea. They can be found along the coast during stormy weather, when they take shelter on rocky beaches and cliffs. In mid-May, razorbills come ashore in large numbers to mate and nest on steep, rocky cliffs. The female usually lays a single egg, which she may place atop some pebbles to help keep it dry. After about 25 days, the egg hatches. The parents bring fish for their chick and, after 15 to 20 days, lead the young razorbilled auk into the northern seas.

Red Avadavat
Amandava amandava

Length: 4 inches
Weight: 1/3 ounce
Diet: mainly seeds
Number of Eggs: 6 to 10

Home: Southeast Asia
Order: Perching birds
Family: Weaverfinches

 Grasslands

 Birds

© MICHEL LEFEVRE / BIOS / PETER ARNOLD, INC.

The beautiful red avadavat is often kept as a cage bird. Its exotic name refers to an ancient Indian city from which the bird was first exported to Europe. Its common name—the strawberry finch— derives from the bright crimson feathers worn by the male during the breeding season. Like a strawberry, his colorful wings and body are speckled with spots. Once breeding season is over, the male's brilliant feathers fade to match those of his mate. The female and nonbreeding male are olive brown with a light gray belly and throat. Both sexes have a flaming red bill and a distinctive red patch at the end of the tail.

In the wild, the red avadavat lives in the swampy grasslands and cultivated rice fields of Southeast Asia. It spends most of the day gleaning, or gathering, seeds on the ground and among tall reeds. A social bird, the avadavat is seldom seen by itself; it prefers to feed in groups of up to 30 birds. Avadavat flocks often intermingle with other types of seed-eating songbirds.

Mated avadavats construct ball-shaped woven nests from long strands of grass. As they weave, the birds suspend their nest between several strong plant stems, leaving a small opening on the side as an entrance. Inside the nest, the female warms a clutch of 6 to 10 eggs. Once the chicks hatch, they are fed soft insects by both of their parents.

Babirusa
Babyrousa babyrussa

Length of the Body: 36 to 42 inches
Length of the Tail: 8 to 12 inches
Diet: leaves, fruits, and insect larvae

Weight: up to 220 pounds
Number of Young: 1 or 2
Home: Indonesia
Order: Even-toed hoofed mammals
Family: Pigs

 Rain forests

Mammals

Endangere
Animals

© ROD WILLIAMS / NATURE PICTURE LIBRARY

The babirusa is a strange-looking pig. In fact, some scientists suggest that babirusas are more closely related to hippopotamuses than to pigs.

A distinguishing feature of the babirusa is its tusks. The two tusks in the male's upper jaw grow straight upward through the skin of the snout, then curve backward, reaching a length of 12 inches or more. The two tusks in the male's lower jaw are shorter, but they, too, grow upward toward the forehead. Female babirusas have much smaller tusks. The purpose of the male's tusks is not clear. The tusks break off easily and therefore are not useful in fighting.

Babirusas live alone or in small family groups. At dusk and during the night, they travel through the Indonesian forests along favorite paths, looking for fruits, leaves, fungi, and other food. Babirusas have longer legs than other pigs and can run remarkably fast. They are also excellent swimmers and will occasionally swim from one island to another!

A baby babirusa weighs 1 to 2 pounds at birth. It feeds on its mother's milk for six to eight months, although it also begins to eat solid food just a few days after birth. The upper tusks of young males begin to grow through the top of the snout when the animals are about 16 months old.

American Badger
Taxidea taxus

Length of the Body: 2 feet
Length of the Tail: 4 to 5 inches
Diet: small mammals, birds, eggs, reptiles, insects, and worms

Weight: up to 26 pounds
Number of Young: 1 to 5
Home: North America
Order: Carnivores
Family: Weasels, badgers, skunks, and otters

 Grasslands

 Mammals

© JEFF VANUGA / CORBIS

The stout and shaggy American badger has few predators—and for good reason! The badger's thick fur, heavy neck muscles, and loose, leathery skin serve as excellent protection from most enemies. Not even a rattlesnake can harm it, unless the snake bites the badger directly on the nose. The badger's teeth and claws are large and sharp. Yet the creature prefers to back away from a fight—hissing, snarling, and growling. When bothered by humans, the badger can dig itself into the ground so quickly that it seems to sink before your eyes.

This powerful digging machine attacks ground squirrels, gophers, rats, and mice by tearing apart their burrows and devouring the prey in their underground homes.

Occasionally the badger wedges itself into the back of an empty burrow and waits for the unlucky occupant to return. Coyotes have learned to follow the badger on its deadly raids. They pounce on any rodent that manages to escape the badger by fleeing out an escape tunnel.

American badgers get along with each other only during the mating season, usually in July. The fertilized eggs inside the female's body do not develop until the following year. Her babies usually arrive in March or April. After raising her family through the summer, the mother leaves them on their own in the fall. American badgers have been known to live more than 15 years.

Common Pipistrelle Bat
Pipistrellus pipistrellus

Length of the Body: 1⅓ to 2 inches
Length of the Forearm: 1 to 1½ inches
Length of the Tail: 1 to 1⅓ inches
Weight: ⅒ to ³⁄₁₀ of an ounce

Diet: small insects
Number of Young: 1 or 2
Home: Europe and northern Africa
Order: Bats
Family: Common bats

Cities, Towns, and Farms

Mammals

AGE FOTOSTOCK / SUPERSTOCK

The common pipistrelle is not only the most abundant bat in Europe, it is also the tiniest. Its body is covered with long grayish-brown fur. Its ears and nose are short and wide. The bat's tail is relatively long compared with its body. Although the pipistrelle is dainty, it is a robust and hearty bat that can withstand cold weather.

During the day, pipistrelles roost in hollow trees and in buildings, especially under roofs. Unlike many bats, this species generally avoids caves. Pipstrelle colonies vary in size from a small handful of bats to several hundred. Often they sleep among larger bats of another species.

Occasionally pipistrelles fly during the day. But like most bats, they are primarily nighttime hunters. Shortly after sunset the bats take to the air. They can nimbly catch small insects, including crane flies and gnats. Pipistrelles locate their prey in the dark by emitting high-pitched sounds through their mouths and then listening for the ultrasonic echoes. This enables the bats to sense the size, shape, and location of objects in their path.

Most of these pipistrelles mate in late May or June; the females give birth in July. In Great Britain, most females have a single baby, but twins are more common in northern and Central Europe.

Fisherman Bat
Noctilio leporinus

Length of the Body: 3 to 5 inches

Length of the Tail: up to 1 inch

Diet: fish, small crustaceans, and insects

Weight: ½ to 2½ ounces

Number of Young: 1

Home: Central and South America and West Indies

Order: Bats

Family: Fisherman bats

Forests and Mountains

Mammals

© STEPHEN DALTON / ANIMALS ANIMALS / EARTH SCENES

The fisherman bat uses its sonarlike sense to detect the ripples made by fish swimming close to the water's surface. When it spots its prey, the fisherman bat swoops low over the water, dunks in its powerful legs and feet, and spears the meaty fish with its sharp, curved toe claws. This aquatic bat is also a strong swimmer that is clever enough to use its broad wings as oars.

The fisherman bat is also called the bulldog bat because its wedge-shaped head and prominent nostrils resemble a bulldog. A gregarious species, it likes to nest with many other fisherman bats and does not even mind sleeping with bats of other species. Fisherman bats spend most of the day clinging to the sides of the caves or hiding in rock crevices and tree holes. They are particularly fond of high cliffs near the seashore. They emerge from their daily snooze in late afternoon and evening, making a beeline for a nearby lake, stream, or bay.

Although it has no natural enemies, the fisherman bat is nonetheless threatened by the destruction of its habitat. People have cut down much of the bat's forest home and polluted the waters in which it fishes. Fortunately, the nations of Central and South America are taking a new interest in their beautiful wildlands. Hopefully, these countries will be able to stop, or even reverse, destructive development and secure the habitat of these peaceful creatures.

Spear-Nosed Bat
Phyllostomus sp.

Length of the Body: 4 to 5¼ inches
Wingspan: about 1½ feet
Weight: up to 3½ ounces
Diet: small animals and fruits
Number of Young: 1

Home: Central and South America
Order: Bats
Family: American leaf-nosed bats

 Rain forests

 Mammals

© RUSSELL C. HANSEN / PETER ARNOLD, INC.

As its name suggests, the spear-nosed bat is equipped with a pointed, triangular flap of skin on its snout. The bat uses this "nose leaf" and a V-shaped groove in its lower lip to direct its high-pitched sounds. Like many bats, spear-noses navigate through the dark by listening to the echoes of their signals.

The spear-nosed bats of Central and South America are most abundant in the rain forest, although they also live in drier woodlands. These large, heavy bats are thickly covered in beautiful fur that ranges in color from dark gray to rusty red. They make their homes in caves or large, hollowed-out trees, where they roost by the hundreds—sometimes even the thousands.

In the evening the colonies rise from their daytime roosts in what appear to be large, dark clouds. Over the past 50 years, humans destroyed many of these roosting sites and thereby reduced the species' numbers.

This creature's diet is quite varied. It will eat anything from tropical fruits to insects, lizards, and rodents. It will even eat smaller bats. Spear-noses are occasionally eaten by an even larger bat, the false vampire bat, *Vampyrum spectrum.*

Most spear-nosed bats mate in fall and give birth in the spring of the following year. The mother nurses her single baby for several months. Scientists estimate that spear-noses live as long as 20 years.

Red Batfish
Halieutaea stellate

Length: up to 1 foot
Diet: small crustaceans and other invertebrates
Method of Reproduction: egg layer

Home: coastal waters from Japan to India
Order: Anglerfishes and their relatives
Family: Batfishes

 Oceans and Shores

 Fish

© STEPHEN FRINK / CORBIS

Walking along the soft, sandy seabed of the South China Sea is a peculiar fish that can barely swim. A fish's pectoral, or front, fins can be compared to human arms, just as their pelvic, or back, fins are somewhat like human legs. The red batfish's fins are more armlike and leglike than most. As a result, it is a poor swimmer, but a good walker. The batfish pulls itself along with its long, stiff front fins. At the same time, it kicks and scoots along with its smaller back fins.

As it wobbles along the seafloor, the red batfish looks for an area where small crabs and other invertebrates are abundant. It then lies very still and tries to tempt its prey with a strange fishing lure. The first spine on the batfish's top fin is so ic̲ ᷉ over the fish's head. There it dang᷉ and lure of a fishing pole. When a ᷉ comes to snap at the wiggling lure, the batfish eats the victim.

The batfish's body is flat, like a pancake with a big tail. When it is picked up out of the water by its sides, it looks much like a bat with its wings outstretched.

When she spawns, the female batfish releases a large, sticky curtain of eggs. The eggs float together with the ocean currents. When the tiny batfish larvae hatch, they, too, drift along for a time. As they mature, the young fish settle to the ocean floor, where they flatten into the shape of their parents.

Grizzly Bear
Ursus arctos horribilis

Length: 7 to 8 feet
Weight: up to 850 pounds
Diet: plants and animals
Number of Young: usually 2

Home: Alaska and western Canada
Order: Carnivores
Family: Bears

 Forests and Mountains

 Mammals

© PAUL A. SOUDERS / CORBIS

Grizzly bears usually mind their own business. But if they or their offspring are threatened, they become fierce fighters. These bears are named for their gray-streaked (grizzled) fur. The fur ranges in color from pale tan to dark brown. In all cases, the tips of the hairs are light gray. Grizzlies are massive animals. Because of their weight, they do not climb trees. Grizzlies are, however, agile on the ground. They move easily through dense forests and across rocky mountains. Their diet is varied and usually includes both plants and animals. These creatures generally move too slowly to catch wild hoofed mammals, but will occasionally kill domestic livestock. In autumn, grizzlies eat enormous amounts of food to fatten up for winter. They hibernate in a cave or other natural shelter or in a den dug in a hillside.

Female grizzlies mate every other year. They usually give birth to one or two young, called cubs. The cubs are very small at birth and stay in the den where they were born until they are about four months old. Then they begin to follow their mother on her daily search for food. The mother cares for her cubs for a year or more.

At one time, grizzles roamed much of western North America, from northern Mexico to Alaska and Canada. Today they are rare. Most remaining grizzlies live in Alaska and Canada, with several hundred living in the northern Rocky Mountains.

Spectacled Bear
Tremarctos ornatus

Weight: 285 to 440 pounds (male); 75 to 145 pounds (female)
Diet: plant matter and small animals

Length: 4 to 7 feet
Number of Young: 1 to 3
Home: South America
Order: Carnivores
Family: Bears

  Forests and Mountains

Mammals

© FRANCOIS SAVIGNY / NATURE PICTURE LIBRARY

Spectacled bears are named for the circles of white fur around their eyes. These circles make the creatures look as if they are wearing eyeglasses—or "spectacles," as they were once called. The spectacled variety are the only bears native to South America. Although they live in many habitats—tropical grasslands, rain forests, and coastal areas—spectacled bears are most common in cool forests high in the Andes Mountains.

During the day, spectacled bears rest under trees or in caves. As the sun begins to set, the bears set out through the forest, searching for food. They have an excellent sense of smell, but, like all bears, their vision and hearing are not very good. Nimble climbers, spectacled bears often go up trees to get fruit, which is their favorite food. They also eat seeds, leaves, palm sprouts, bamboo hearts, and an occasional rodent or insect. Sometimes a spectacled bear builds a large platform of broken branches in a tree. It uses the platform as a resting place and a spot from which to reach fruit that would otherwise be out of reach.

Spectacled bears live alone or in small family groups consisting of a mother and her young. Young bears, called cubs, stay with their mother until they are fully grown. She teaches the cubs how to find food, and other skills they need to survive.

European Bee-Eater
Merops apiaster

Length: 11 inches
Weight: 2 ounces
Number of Eggs: usually 4 to 7
Diet: insects

Home: Europe, Asia, and Africa
Order: Kingfishers and their relatives
Family: Bee-eaters

 Grasslands

 Birds

© FRANCESC MUNTADA / CORBIS

The European bee-eater is an expert at catching its favorite foods: bees, wasps, and hornets. The bird swoops gracefully through the air and captures its prey in flight. Then it flies to a nearby tree and beats the insect against a tree branch over and over again, until the insect's stinger no longer works. Finally the insect is tossed up into the air, caught in the bee-eater's beak, and swallowed headfirst.

European bee-eaters are sociable animals and often breed in large colonies. Although these birds live in treetops, they nest in the ground. The male and female take turns digging a tunnel in the soil. They use their beak to loosen the soil, then scratch the soil away with their feet. They dig a nesting chamber at the end of the tunnel and try to make the chamber higher than the entrance to the tunnel. This helps to prevent rainwater from flooding the nesting chamber and killing the bee-eaters' eggs or baby birds.

The parent bee-eaters take turns incubating, or sitting on, the eggs and caring for the young birds. The newly hatched babies, weighing only $\frac{1}{10}$ of an ounce, are born naked and unable to see. Feathers begin to appear on the fifth day of life, and the babies open their eyes on the sixth day.

Bee-eaters that spend the summer in temperate areas, such as Central and northern Europe, migrate southward to spend the winter in warmer places.

Goliath Beetle
Goliathus sp.

Length: up to 5 inches
Wingspan: 2 inches
Method of Reproduction: egg layer

Diet: nectar, pollen, and sap
Home: Africa
Order: Beetles
Family: Scarab beetles

 Rain forests

 Arthropods

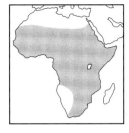

© E. R. DEGGINGER / COLOR-PIC INC.

Nearly the size of a baseball, the goliath beetle zooms through the treetops of the African jungle. It is named for the biblical giant Goliath and is easily recognized by the shiny black markings on its grayish-white back. Many species of goliath beetle are sought by collectors because of their large size, dramatic markings, and velvety body. The males are especially valued for their large, dramatic horns. But the beetle's body is easily damaged by rough handling, so few collectors have perfect or whole specimens.

In the rain forests of Africa, goliath beetles fly at great heights, using only their hind wings. The front wings, called "elytra," are hard and do not open from side to side.

The beetle can raise its elytra just high enough to allow its back wings to spread for flight. Goliath beetles feed on flowers and sap at the tops of palms and other blossoming trees. They seldom come to the ground.

After mating, the female lays her eggs in rotting wood. The eggs hatch into wormlike larvae, called grubs, that eat hungrily and grow rapidly. As the grub grows, it sheds its stiff skin like outgrown clothes. The grub "molts" in this way five or six times before it is full grown. After it has eaten its fill, the larva becomes a motionless pupa. In this "sleeping" stage, it transforms into a winged adult.

Red Poplar Leaf Beetle
Melasoma populi

Length: up to ½ inch
Diet: leaves of poplar, aspen, and willow trees
Method of Reproduction: egg layer

Home: Europe and Great Britain
Order: Beetles
Family: Leaf beetles

 Forests and Mountains

 Arthropods

© HANS PFLETSCHINGER / PETER ARNOLD, INC.

There are more than 37,000 species of leaf beetles around the world, the smallest being the size of a flea, and the largest about an inch long. The ½-inch red poplar leaf beetle is one of Europe's largest. Leaf beetles all fly very well. They also share a similar body build: chubby and round, with short antennae.

The red poplar leaf beetle's marvelous color attracts attention. If you were to look very closely, you would see that its head and thorax, or shoulders, are a beautiful metallic green, while its underside is black.

The adult female lays her eggs on the leaves of young poplar bushes, aspens, and willows. When they are born, the immature larvae are pale pink. The larvae are hard to spot in the thick summer foliage, but it is easy to recognize their handiwork. They eat all the juicy parts of a leaf, leaving behind only a lacy skeleton of veins.

When it is bothered, the larva produces droplets of liquid from glands on its back. The droplets may taste bad to predators such as birds and larger insects. When things have quieted down, the larva reabsorbs the liquid into its body. When it is time to "pupate," or turn into an adult beetle, the larva crawls under an uneaten leaf. There it emerges as an adult 10 days later. In winter, adult leaf beetles hibernate.

Scarlet Fire Beetle
Pyrochroa sp.

Diet: flowers (adult); wood and small insects (larva)
Method of Reproduction: egg layer

Length: up to ¾ inch
Home: Europe
Order: Beetles
Family: Cardinal beetles

 Forests and Mountains

 Arthropods

© MARTIN DOHRN / NATURE PICTURE LIBRARY

Scarlet fire beetles are a brilliant red and black. They belong to a small family of beetles—the cardinal beetles—recognized by their scarlet color and long, rectangular shape. Most scarlet fire beetles have a shiny black head, but some are yellow- or redheaded. The male can be recognized by his jagged, almost feathery-looking antennae. Three species of scarlet fire beetle (genus *Pyrochroa*) thrive in and around the wooded parts of Europe. A closely related cousin, the fire-colored beetle, *Dendroides bicolor*, lives in North America, but it is not common.

In June, adult scarlet fire beetles nibble on flowers at the forest edge. They fly from plant to plant during the warm summer season. After mating, the female lays her eggs under the bark of old tree stumps. When they hatch, the immature larvae, or "grubs," look like small worms. They remain under the tree bark for two or three years; during this time they eat wood and prey on other insects and their larvae. Sometimes the grubs eat each other.

In the spring of their third year, the grubs hide inside rotten wood and spin a cocoon around themselves. Fourteen days later, they emerge as adult fire beetles. Their lifespan is short—adult scarlet fire beetles survive only one season.

Stag Beetle
Lucanus cervus

Length: 1½ to 3 inches (male);
1¼ to 1¾ inches (female)
Diet: decayed wood
Method of Reproduction: egg
layer

Home: central and southern
Europe; Morocco, Algeria,
and Tunisia
Order: Beetles
Family: Stag beetles

Forests and
Mountains

Arthropods

© DEREK MIDDLETON / FRANK LANE PICTURE AGENCY / CORBIS

The stag beetle is brown or black, but it is still very easy to spot. The male is very large—up to 3 inches long. Its giant pincers, or mandibles, have points that look like a stag's antlers—that is where this beetle gets its name.

In June and July, stag beetles can be found in the woods. At dusk, males fly over trees looking for females that cling to tree trunks. The male flies fast in an almost straight up-and-down pattern to balance the weight of his pincers. These amazing pincers have two purposes: to attract females and to fight other males. When they fight, the males try to grab each other with their pincers, and each tries to turn the other one over. Once turned over, the insect will die. Sometimes they punch holes in the coverings that protect their wings. The female lays her eggs in an old, worm-eaten oak. The eggs transform into the larval stage. The larva grows for four or five years, feeding on rotted wood. After this growth period, it buries itself in the ground close to a tree while it turns into the next stage, called a nymph. The adult stag beetle is formed by fall, but it waits until the next summer to come out into the open air. It lives as an adult for only four weeks.

There are approximately 900 types of stag beetles in the world. Some of them have pincers as long as their bodies.

30

Tiger Beetle
Cicindela sp.

Length: ½ to ¾ inch
Diet: other insects
Home: North America, Europe, Central Asia, and northern Africa

Method of Reproduction: egg layer
Order: Beetles
Family: Tiger beetles

 Forests and Mountains

 Arthropods

© N. CATTLIN / HOLT STUDIOS INTERNATIONAL / PHOTO RESEARCHERS

Tiger beetles earn their name both by their fearsomeness and their markings. Some species have stripes and bars as distinctive as any true tiger. In general, tiger beetles are very colorful. The splendid tiger beetle, *C. splendida*, of eastern North America has metallic green wing covers with sparkling blue edges. The bronze tiger beetle, *C. repanda*, is shiny brown with green and coppery highlights. It is found throughout the United States and southern Canada.

Like true tigers, the adult tiger beetle races quickly after its prey and kills with a powerful bite. It can also fly with great speed. The immature tiger beetle, or larva, is as fearsome as its parents. It digs a burrow straight down into the soil. Then the larva plugs the opening of its hole with its body and holds its powerful jaws wide open. When a passing insect steps into the trap, the larva's jaws snap shut. If the insect prey is large, a tremendous struggle may follow. Finally the victim is pulled into the tiger beetle larva's burrow and is eaten.

Because of their brilliant colors, adult tiger beetles are among the most prized insects in "bug" collections. Fortunately for the beetle, it is fast and agile and almost impossible to catch! Should you somehow manage to catch it, the tiger beetle may still escape because it can deliver a painful bite to your hand.

Secretary Bird
Sagittarius serpentarius

Height: 4½ feet
Diet: insects, birds, rodents, and reptiles
Number of Eggs: 2 or 3

Home: sub-Saharan Africa
Order: Birds of prey
Family: The secretary bird

 Grasslands

 Birds

© ROGER WILMSHURST / FRANK LANE PICTURE AGENCY / CORBIS

Two hundred years ago, clerks and secretaries kept their writing instruments—goose-quill pens—stuck in their wigs. When a strange bird was discovered with black feathers stuck on its neck like goose quills in a wig, it was named the "secretary bird." Today in Europe it is also commonly called "the serpent eater," because it eats snakes.

The secretary bird lives in the savannas of the southern half of Africa between the Sahara Desert and the Cape of Good Hope. It stays in open places, but it also ventures into farming land. Perched on its stiltlike legs, it searches the ground for rodents, its favorite prey. As soon as it sees one, it grabs the victim with its beak, holds it

firmly to the ground with its feet, and smashes the skull with its powerful beak. When it spots a snake, it kills it by stamping on it with its feet. The bird's long legs put its body out of reach of snakes' fangs. It also eats insects, birds, and lizards.

The bird's wingspread can be almost 6½ feet. It can soar and fly swiftly in the air, even though it spends most of its time on the ground. It spends nights at the top of trees and comes down at daybreak to hunt.

The secretary bird builds a nest at the top of an acacia tree. The female sits on the nest, but both parents tend their young. At 2½ months, the chicks begin to fly and abandon the nest to learn to hunt with their parents.

European Blackbird
Turdus merula

Length: 10 inches
Weight: 2½ to 4 ounces
Diet: insects and fruits
Number of Eggs: 3 to 5

Home: Eurasia and northern Africa
Order: Perching birds
Family: Thrushes

 Forests and Mountains

 Birds

© ERIC AND DAVID HOSKING / CORBIS

The European blackbird is found in most of Europe, in parts of North Africa, Central Asia, India, China, Australia, and New Zealand. In the past, it lived only in the forest. The black feathers of the male and the brownish feathers of the female and the young make them nearly invisible.

Even though blackbirds spend a lot of time on the ground finding food, they usually build their nests in bushes and shrubs. In the forest, they choose low bushes and prefer blackberry bushes. In lake regions, they build their nests among the reeds. In open fields, they nest in thick hedges. In the cities, hedges in parks and gardens provide ideal nesting places. Even thick ivy growing up the side of a wall may do. Blackbirds living in cities and villages are less fearful and also more careless than their forest cousins. They often nest where cats can get at their young.

The blackbird's diet is varied. It eats all kinds of insects, larvae, spiders, and earthworms. At the end of the summer when wild fruit is ripe, blackbirds stuff themselves with sweet and juicy berries.

The male, with his black feathers, yellow beak, and black eyes ringed with yellow, is a beautiful songster. Starting in February, you can hear his marvelous songs at dawn and at dusk. The closer it is to mating season, the more intense and pure is the song.

Blackdevil
Melanocetus johnsoni

Length: up to 4⅜ inches
Diet: lanternfish and other deep-sea fish
Method of Reproduction: egg layer

Home: Atlantic, Indian, and Pacific oceans
Order: Anglerfishes and their relatives
Family: Melanocetids

 Oceans and Shores

 Fish

© E. WIDDER / HBOI / VISUALS UNLIMITED

The strange blackdevil is a rare type of anglerfish that lives in deep, remote areas of the ocean. Occasionally one is accidentally caught in the large nets of commercial fishing boats.

Actually, it is only the female blackdevil that is such a bizarre-looking fish. When they first hatch, females and males look very much alike. However, by the time the young female is an inch long, her unscaled skin has darkened to black, and she has grown large, sharp fangs and a tentacle between her eyes. The female's tentacle is a fishing lure with a "light bulb" at the end. In the darkness of the deep ocean, other fish are attracted to the light. The female blackdevil lures her prey right into her gaping mouth. Because her body is so fat and round, she can swallow fish longer than herself.

In most species of anglerfish, the male never eats. He just hangs on to the female's body with his toothless mouth. After mating, he dies. The male blackdevil does seem to feed, although only on fish lice and tiny shrimp. However, his main mission in life is to find a female. For this duty, he is equipped with very large eyes and a keen sense of smell. He is also an excellent swimmer and can move much faster than his oddly shaped mate. Once he finds a female, the male blackdevil anchors himself to her side with a small bite. When the female eventually sheds her eggs, her hitchhiking mate fertilizes them.

Bleak
Alburnus alburnus

Length: 4 to 8 inches
Diet: plankton, insects, and baby fish
Method of Reproduction: egg layer

Home: Europe and Asia
Order: Carps and their relatives
Family: Minnows

Fresh Water

Fish

© LUTRA / NHPA / PHOTO RESEARCHERS

In Europe the bleak is often seen splashing near the water's surface along riverbanks and lakeshores. This lively little minnow gathers in large schools. History books tell of enormous numbers of bleaks, with as many as 8 million to 10 million fish in a single school. Because of their abundance, bleaks were once harvested from the water by the tens of thousands. In years past, some people used the fish only for its silvery scales, which flake off easily from its body. Beadmakers rolled the fishy flakes into inexpensive, artificial pearls. Nature lovers decried the large-scale slaughter as wasteful.

Today bleaks are caught in smaller numbers. They can be eaten by humans, but bleak flesh is very bony. In nature, bleaks are important as food for larger fish. European pike, perch, and trout all depend on bleaks for their survival.

April through July is mating season for the bleak. During this time the adult males grow small white bumps on their head and back. The females gather over shallow, gravelly areas in a river, where they spread their eggs. Once laid and fertilized, the eggs stick firmly to stones and plants. Two to three weeks later, the eggs hatch into tiny fish, called fry, that are no bigger than your small fingernail. By the time the young fish are a year old, they are about an inch and a half long. They continue to grow about an inch a year for as long as seven years.

Indian Bloodsucker
Calotes versicolor

Length: 12 to 19½ inches
Diet: mainly insects and spiders
Number of Eggs: 4 to 23

Home: southern Asia
Order: Lizards and snakes
Family: Chisel-teethed lizards

 Rain forests

 Reptiles

© PREMAPHOTOS / NATURE PICTURE LIBRARY

Despite its name, the Indian bloodsucker is no vampire. But the male of this species does undergo some frightening color changes. When excited, his head and shoulders become bright red. During mating season, this red color becomes even more brilliant. In fact, this lizard looks as though it has dipped its head in blood! In truth, the Indian bloodsucker's only bloodthirsty habit is to occasionally snatch a baby bird from a nest. Usually this common tree lizard helps keep pests under control by eating insects and spiders.

During breeding season, the bright red male Indian bloodsucker performs a solemn courtship dance. Once he has found a female, he stands before her, opening and closing his mouth and nodding his blood-red head up and down. At the same time, he puffs out his throat like a balloon. If she is impressed, the female will allow the male to fertilize her eggs.

Indian bloodsuckers of both sexes change colors when basking in the sun, as well as when frightened or angry. The chameleonlike change—from bright green to reddish brown—is caused by a rise in the lizard's body temperature. A frightened bloodsucker may also twitch its long, slender tail. Often a predator will bite the bloodsucker's twitching tail instead of its body. Then the lizard has a good chance of escaping alive and growing a new tail.

Red-Headed Blowfly
Calliphora erythrocephala

Diet: plant nectar, feces, and the juices of rotting flesh
Method of Reproduction: egg layer

Length: ½ inch
Home: worldwide
Order: Flies and mosquitoes
Family: Blowflies

 Grasslands

 Arthropods

© A. SHAY / OSF / ANIMALS ANIMALS / EARTH SCENES

Red-headed blowflies have habits that make them unwelcome in any home or farm building. These pests frantically fly from place to place, searching for meat on which to feed. Outdoors, red-headed blowflies like nothing better than to crawl on dung and dead animals. Blowflies can carry bacteria that cause such human diseases as cholera, anthrax, and dysentery. As the red-headed blowflies feed, they deposit bacteria on the food. If people eat the same food—such as a piece of meat—they can be infected with the bacteria.

Like its relative, *C. vomitoria*, the red-headed blowfly is often called the bluebottle because of its metallic-blue body. The sides of its head are reddish-orange, and its two transparent wings are strengthened by dark structures called veins.

There are four stages in the life cycle of a red-headed blowfly: egg, larva, pupa, and adult. The female lays large batches of eggs on raw meat. In just one day, the eggs hatch into white, wormlike larvae called maggots. The maggots dig into the meat and produce a digestive juice that breaks down the flesh, turning it into a liquid, which the maggots lap up. When the maggots are a week old, they crawl out of the meat and find a dry place in which to pupate. During the pupa stage, the maggots metamorphose, or change, into adults. This process takes about a week.

Boomslang
Dispholidus typus

Length: 4 to 6½ feet
Diet: lizards and birds
Number of Eggs: 10 to 25

Home: sub-Saharan Africa
Order: Lizards and snakes
Family: Colubrid snakes

 Forests and Mountains

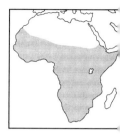

 Reptiles

© ANTHONY BANNISTER / GALLO IMAGES / CORBIS

The boomslang belongs to a family of snakes that are often called the "harmless snakes." But this species certainly is not harmless! Luckily, the large, deadly boomslang is by nature unaggressive toward humans. That is to say, it will not go out of its way to bite. But bother the boomslang, and it may not hesitate to strike you. Just a drop of its venom is enough to kill. The poison makes the victim's blood very "thin," so that he or she bleeds to death internally.

Fortunately, most native Africans know to avoid the boomslang and can recognize the snake by its brightly colored neck skin. When cornered, the boomslang warns its enemy by raising its head and inflating its neck. The boomslang's prey are not as lucky. This snake is a lively hunter that races after lizards and birds through grass and up into trees. In addition to speed, the snake has the advantage of keen vision.

While female boomslangs wear drab brown scales, the male comes in a variety of bright colors. Some are leaf-green with a paler green belly. Others are yellow with black-edged scales and a speckled head. A third comes in red with an orange-pink belly.

Female boomslangs lay their eggs during the summer, carefully hiding them in high tree hollows or among fallen leaves on the ground. When they hatch, the newborn boomslangs are already poisonous.

Bullfinch
Pyrrhula pyrrhula

Length: 5½ to 6¼ inches
Weight: ¾ to 1 ounce
Diet: buds, berries, and seeds
Number of Eggs: 4 or 5

Home: Europe and Asia
Order: Perching birds
Family: Finches

Forests and Mountains

Birds

© UWE WALZ / CORBIS

The male bullfinch is a striking bird with rosy-colored cheeks and breast and a bluish-gray back. Both sexes have a handsome black cap, dark wings and tail, and a stubby black beak. The female is gray with a pinkish-brown breast. All young bullfinches resemble their mothers. The bird's name dates back many centuries and probably refers to the finch's thick (bull-like) neck.

The bullfinch is much loved for its warbling song, "teek, teek, tioooo," a mixture of melodious notes and creaking noises. The bird is often kept as a pet and can be taught to whistle simple tunes. In the wild, it is quite shy and hides in the trees, seldom settling on the ground. Overall, the world's bullfinches are doing well.

However, one subspecies—the São Miguel bullfinch of the Azores (off the coast of Portugal)—is in danger of extinction.

Bullfinches can be troublesome to humans. In springtime, they feed on tender buds of fruit trees. Large flocks can cause considerable damage to orchards and gardens. Bullfinches also eat buds of other trees. Later in the summer, they feast on berries and seeds.

The male's bright colors and lively song are important during courtship. The showiest males have the best chance of winning a mate. After breeding, the female builds a nest of twigs and moss in an evergreen tree or a bush. She incubates the eggs and feeds the chicks without any help from the male.

Snow Bunting
Plectrophenax nivalis

Length: 6 to 7¼ inches
Number of Eggs: 4 to 7
Home: *Summer:* Arctic
   Winter: North America and
   Europe

Diet: seeds, spiders, and small
   crustaceans
Order: Perching birds
Family: Buntings and
   American sparrows

 Arctic and Anarctic

 Birds

☐ Summer
☐ Winter

© NIALL BENVIE / CORBIS

While many of the world's birds are brightly colored, the snow bunting demonstrates that even a colorless bird can be striking. The male snow bunting is particularly dashing in summer. His pure white coat is etched with black highlights atop his wingtips and tail feathers. In winter a flock of snow buntings high above a field might easily be mistaken for a cloud of swirling snowflakes.

In early spring the male snow bunting flies north to the Arctic. The female catches up about a month later. Then it is time for courtship. First, the male catches a female's attention by standing erect with his tail and wings widely spread. Then he turns his tail and runs from her. Of course, if the female does not follow, her suitor quickly returns and repeats the sequence again.

Once they have mated, a snow-bunting couple scratches out a nest in the frozen tundra—perhaps beneath a rock or in a pile of stones. They line this shallow hole with bits of grass, moss, lichen, and the soft fuzz of pussy willows. The mother bird lays her speckled green eggs one at a time over several days. As the female sits on the nest, her mate flies to the beach and fetches juicy mollusks and crabs for her to eat. Once the first hatchling is born, its brothers and sisters follow a day or two apart. Just two weeks after hatching, the young birds are ready to fly and form their own "teenage" flock.

Burbot
Lota lota

Length: up to 33 inches
Diet: smaller fish, fish eggs, and invertebrates
Number of Eggs: 45,000 to 1 million

Weight: up to 18¼ pounds
Home: North America, Europe, and Asia
Order: Cod and their relatives
Family: Cod

Fresh Water

Fish

© HUGO WILLOCX / FOTO NATURA / MINDEN PICTURES

The burbot, the world's only freshwater codfish, lives in North America, Europe, and Asia. A rather eccentric creature, the burbot dislikes both light and warmth. During the day, it hides under a rock slab or a submerged tree, or inside an underground tunnel. In midsummer, when lakes and rivers are warm, the burbot barely moves at all. But on cold winter nights, this fish becomes a fast-moving, aggressive hunter. Its appetite is most voracious between December and March, when lakes and rivers are covered with ice.

Male and female burbot pause from their winter feeding frenzy only long enough to mate. Their spawning occurs late at night in January or February, when the water is at its most frigid. Moving in groups of 10 or 12, the females shed their eggs over gravel. The males follow behind to fertilize them. The eggs slowly sink to the lake or river bottom, hatching about a month later.

Young burbot are ready to mate when they are three or four years old. They continue to grow as long as they live. Lake burbot grow faster and live longer than do river burbot. Burbot in Lake Erie are about 2 feet long by age 10 and may live another 10 years after that. In contrast, burbot in the Susquehanna River of New York grow no bigger than 14 inches and live, at most, seven years. The largest burbot ever caught came from the Onega Sea of Russia: it was 3½ feet long and weighed 50 pounds!

Senegal Bushbaby (Lesser Bushbaby)
Galago senegalensis

Length of the Body: 5½ to 7½ inches
Length of the Tail: 9 to 12 inches
Diet: mainly insects and tree sap

Weight: 5 to 15 ounces
Number of Young: 1; rarely 2
Home: Africa
Order: Primates
Family: Bushbabies

  Grasslands

Mammals

© MARTIN HARVEY / GALLO IMAGES / CORBIS

The bushbaby is not named for its adorable, babyish appearance, but rather for its nighttime cries that sound like the wails of a human baby. The Senegal, or lesser, bushbaby is one of the smaller of six species of bushbaby that live in central and southern Africa. And only the Senegal bushbaby makes its home in the dry gallery forests of the savanna; its cousins stay in the jungle. To most people, the Senegal species is the most familiar member of its family because it is often raised in zoos.

This primate is covered with silky, soft fur. Most individuals are gray or brown with a cream-colored stripe between the eyes. The toes and fingers are short with padded tips and long nails that enable the animal to cling tightly to tree branches. Its long, powerful back legs are designed for jumping. A Senegal bushbaby standing on the ground can leap onto a branch 7 feet above its head—more than 10 times its own height.

Senegal bushbabies sleep during the day, huddled in large family groups. At night they hunt through the trees, usually singly or in pairs. Their large ears enable them to hear the movements of tiny grasshoppers and other insects. A newborn bushbaby will usually accompany its mother on the hunt, clinging tightly to her back. Youngsters become independent when they are about 10 weeks old.

Kori Bustard
Ardeotis kori

Length: 3 to 4 feet
Weight: to 30 pounds
Diet: insects, small animals, seeds, plant shoots, fruit
Number of Eggs: 1 to 4

Home: northeast and southern Africa (two populations)
Order: Cranes, rails, and relatives
Family: Bustards

Grasslands

Birds

© CLEM HAAGNER / GALLO IMAGES / CORBIS

This large bustard is about the size of a turkey. It has dark feathers on the back of its head, a long, straight neck, and a long, thin beak. The kori bustard moves on its tall legs over grassy plains. It lowers its head to the ground from time to time to look for seeds or tender plant shoots, insects, or small animals. Often, a smaller bird, the carmine bee-eater, sits on the kori's back and catches insects that the kori misses or does not want.

The kori bustard moves calmly through herds of large animals that travel the African savanna. On the other hand, the kori mistrusts people: it is impossible to get closer than about 2,500 feet to a kori.

To get the female's attention at mating time, the male lifts his tail feathers to show an all-white rump that contrasts with the gray-brownish feathers on the rest of his body. As he comes closer to his future mate, he breathes in the air to swell his neck and makes deep sounds. Once the male finds its mate, they are partners for life.

The female does not build a nest; she lays her eggs on the ground, in the grass, or in a small hollow of a tree. She sits on them for about 20 days. When they hatch, the young are very active. They immediately leave the nest. However, they stay under the protection of their mother until they are able to fly.

Giant Swallowtail Butterfly
Heraclides cresphontes

Wingspan: 3⅜ to 5½ inches
Diet: flower nectar
Method of Reproduction: egg layer

Home: North America
Order: Butterflies and moths
Family: True butterflies

 Cities, Towns, and Farms

 Arthropods

© TOM BRAKEFIELD / CORBIS

There are several species of swallowtail butterfly, all of them unusually large and dramatically marked. With a wingspan of nearly half a foot, the giant swallowtail is the biggest. It is even bigger than some birds!

Giant swallowtails are often seen moving through a citrus grove like a flock of fat yellow ribbons. As they sip nectar, the butterflies help fertilize the citrus blossoms and ensure a good fruit crop. Farmers would like the giant swallowtail better if not for its pesty caterpillar, or immature form. This caterpillar has a bright orange-to-red collar on the back of its neck. It has a voracious appetite for the leaves of both fruit-bearing and ornamental citrus trees.

The caterpillar's brightly colored collar is actually a gland called an "osmeterium." The gland emits a foul-smelling odor when pierced. Once a predator has bitten into one of these "stink glands," it will be discouraged from attacking another orange caterpillar for a long, long time.

In fall, each caterpillar dangles from a twig or leaf and encases its body in silken gray-and-brown threads. This "chrysalis" resembles a dried bit of leaf or wood that hangs motionless through the winter. Although it appears to be lifeless, the chrysalis is full of biological activity. Inside, the wintering caterpillar is transforming into a gorgeous giant swallowtail.